MW00772972

Jill D'Aubery

I must admit, I'm not a reader. However, I started and did not stop until I was done. THANK YOU SO MUCH!
  ~ Tammy Jinks

Thank you for sharing your story, it was raw, compelling, and inspiring. I think this piece is a great celebration of life, for both you and Ben.
  ~Sarah-Ruth Tasko

"I felt like I just had a long, wonderful conversation with you. I love your personal, conversational style."
  ~Lea Semalina

Jill D'Aubery

ESCAPE THE

QUICKSAND OF GRIEF

My Path From Grief Through Sorrow To Joy

Jill D'Aubery

DEDICATION

To those who suffer with grief.

And to my husband, Ben. I will love you forever.

SECTIONS

Jill D'Aubery

WHAT IS GRIEF

WHAT IS GRIEF

The prevailing thought about grieving these days is this: Grief never goes away. You never "get over it." There is no end to grief. You just have to learn to live with it. You have to accept your "new normal" of sadness. All the while putting on a brave face.

While it's true that grief never goes away, think about this for a second: neither does any other emotion that you have ever experienced. Every emotion you have ever felt is still a part of you and always will be. The thrill of a marriage proposal, the excitement of a roller coaster ride, the horror of being fired from a job you need, the wonder you felt when a little wild animal trusted you enough to take a tidbit from your hand…literally thousands of emotions are a part of you. In fact, they really make up who you are. This is the basis of great acting and why Meryl Streep, arguably the finest actress of all time, shines so brilliantly on the silver screen. She can reach inside of herself and find whatever emotion that she has experienced in the past that the character she is portraying is feeling now and then fearlessly let that emotion show for all the world to see and experience for themselves.

So, yes, once it's there, your grief will always be a part of you and, yes, you can survive it. And, yes, you can learn to live with it and make it your new normal. But you can also go deeper, or perhaps higher, and find joy as well since both emotions already exist within you.

Grief is a part of the human condition. So is joy. And everything in between. We go to school to learn the basics of how to function in our world, but there are no formal classes on how to deal with grief. Yet, if you google "grief" you'll find that there are almost as many ways of dealing with it as there are types of grief.

We feel grief when our kids grow up and leave home, but buried inside that grief is the joy of being able to transform the kid's room into a personal gym or library. There is a fleeting grief that some of us feel when a TV show that we just love is canceled, but we can still enjoy the show when it streams, and there will probably be a different show that we will find and love. There is grief when a marriage goes sour or when something we cared about is lost or destroyed.

The deepest kind of grief is about death. From the death of a pet to the death of a child, and that is the grief that I'm going to talk about in this book. Losing someone you love, and love deeply, to death is perhaps the hardest thing you will ever do. And surviving that grief is monumental. It takes enormous amounts of strength right at the very time in your life when you are at your weakest. It requires self-love to an extent that you never thought or wanted possible. It feels agonizing, insurmountable, unbearable. And to think that there is some kind of joy buried inside that overwhelming grief just feels wrong, it feels almost like a betrayal. Like you didn't love the one you lost enough. Like you're not entitled to ever again be happy.

Think about what grief is for a moment. Grief is always about loss. It's the emotional response to losing someone or something. And it's also always about being out of control, about not being able to keep the loss from happening in the first place. When my husband Ben died, I beat myself up over and over by thinking, "I couldn't save him. I wasn't good enough to save him."

We grieve for grandma when she dies. At least we think we're grieving for grandma, but we are really grieving for ourselves. We grieve because we will never again see or talk with or hug grandma, but that's not about grandma, it's about ourselves. When we grieve, we grieve for ourselves not for whoever died.

I've lived with the concept of having a back door for most of my life. I've always had an escape route planned and ready so that when something went south, I could easily and safely leave. A bad love affair? Run. There's always someone new somewhere. A job I hate or a boss making passes at me? No problem, I'd just quit. There was always another job out there. If I quit because the boss was making passes, I also made sure that he knew why I was quitting…and so did everyone else in the company. I doubt that said bosses would do that again. Nonetheless, no matter what the situation was, I always had a way out if I needed it.

But there is no back door for death. There is no escape route. Someone you love has died and you can't change it. You can't bring that loved person back to life.

So, for someone like me, who was used to being able to change anything that had gone wrong by either making it right or simply running away from it, being faced with the incontrovertible truth that my husband had died and there was nothing I could do about it, well, it nearly destroyed me. But I found my way back to life, at least to my life. And to joy.

Here is the path I found that let me walk from the darkness of overwhelming grief into the bright sunshine of joy.

This is my Ben

Teenage Ben

THE GRIEF

CHAPTER ONE

The day my husband died was the first lovely day of Spring after a long, dreary Winter. He had been ill for quite a while but I was still unprepared for the phone call that told me he was gone.

Ben had fallen in the middle of the night and wound up in the hospital with his pelvis broken in two places. He was in a lot of pain and his body started shutting down. He had a heart attack in the hospital a couple of nights later but he made it through that and his heart started working properly again. He was kind of aware and kind of not aware. All in all, it was a pretty awful three days that he spent in the hospital this time.

He had been in the hospital four years before this and survived even though I had been told that he wouldn't. At that time, he had somehow blown a hole in his colon and was, according to the doctors, too fragile for them to operate. Because of this hole, he had body-wide sepsis and they had given him a ton of antibiotics to fight the infection. And all those antibiotics had resulted in something called, *Clostridioides difficile* or *C. Diff* for short. This is an extremely dangerous infection caused by antibiotics killing off most if not all of the good bacteria in our guts that keeps the C. Diff bacteria from taking over in the first place. C. Diff causes deadly diarrhea and an inflamed colon. C. Diff is also highly contagious, it can be passed along by touching something that has C. Diff bacteria on it, and it has a special affinity for people over the age of 65.

My poor Ben already had a colon that was in trouble and with C. Diff added to the mix, the doctors told me that he didn't have much of a chance. They gave him three days to live, at most. But they also gave him a tiny chance: if his own body could grow enough cells to wall off the hole that could not be repaired with surgery, he would live.

And that's exactly what his body did! It grew enough cells to seal off the hole. And grew them quickly. Then a different antibiotic took care of the C. Diff and amazingly three days later instead of dying he was released from the hospital into rehab.

He remembered none of this…he thought he had been on a cruise ship for a few days in the Caribbean! The mind is a fascinating thing.

Because of this prior experience four years before, I was truly stunned when I got the phone call even though I had been told by a doctor earlier that day that he wasn't going to make it. Again, he had been given two to three days to live. But he had survived before, surely he would do so again. That's what my heart said, but my head was different. This time my head knew it was real, that he was not going to live past two or three days.

The call itself was harsh and I didn't know how to process it. That's the thing, there are no classes on How to

Handle the Death of a Loved One, and busy doctors don't have time to deal with the shocked grief of those left behind. They do their best, but that's not enough to make things any easier.

This particular doctor, a Resident, sounded uncomfortable on the phone and clearly did not want to make this call, but someone above his pay grade had given him an order and he had no choice. And no training about how to do such a thing.

The call went like this:

Doctor: Hello, is this Mrs. Jill D'Aubery?

Me: Yes

D: This is Doctor So-and-so. I'm a Resident at the hospital and I've been tasked to call and tell you that your husband has passed.

M: What? No. That can't be. He had two or three days. You mean, he's dead?

D: Yes. You can come up and see him if you like. You can sit with his body for a couple of hours.

M: *(Trying to understand what he was saying.)* Yes. All right. Wait. No. I don't think I can drive right now.

D: Okay. Oh, about the autopsy. Did you want Bennett autopsied?

I said I didn't and the doctor said something about being sorry for my loss and hung up. That was it. Brief. To the point. And utterly devastating.

I looked around our apartment. It hadn't changed, but I had changed. In just a couple of minutes, I was no longer a Wife...I was a Widow. The place where Ben always sat to watch TV was empty and would stay empty. The water bottle that he kept in the fridge would stay full and most of the food would go bad because I simply didn't have the energy or the interest in cooking or eating.

There were phone calls to make and I must have made them although I don't remember dialing the phone. His family was as heartbroken and devastated as I was and the tears flowed from them. My own tears would take a little while because I was in shock. Part of me refused to believe what the doctor had told me, and part of me insisted that it was some kind of macabre mistake, that Ben would phone me any minute and ask me to bring a book to the hospital for him.

And I still had more family to phone and their tears to wade through.

The anger came after the second phone call from the hospital, this one from the nurse that had taken such good care of Ben for the couple of days he had been in her care. The first call, the one from the busy doctor had badly shaken me and left me feeling empty and guilty. The nurse's call went a long way to alleviate the guilt and helped to fill in some of the emptiness. But her call also made me realize, and realize fully, just how awful the doctor's call had been. That's where the anger came in.

The nurse did everything right on her call; she said that she wanted me to know that Ben had not been alone when he died, that she had been with him, holding his hand. That helped so much because I had left him in the hospital to go home and get some paperwork dealt with and take care of our cats, so I was not with him at the most important time of his life and I felt that powerfully.

Then she asked if I wanted to know the particulars. She didn't assume either way, she asked. She also told me that from her experience as a trauma nurse, people often somehow managed to wait to die until their family was not in the room. She didn't know how they did this, or why, but she said it was very common.

Ben and I were close, as close as two people can be. We often finished each other's sentences, we spoke for each other, we trusted each other completely, and we never gave a thought to being apart. Most people thought of us as one person. It was never just Ben or just Jill, it was always Ben&Jill. Yet, here we were…at least, here I was. Alone. Alone and empty. And without a single clue about how to continue living.

I don't remember very much about those first two or three weeks after he died. Somehow, I did my days and even slept at night. Having two cats to care for helped because they needed me, so I had to be at least somewhat present for them. Flowers arrived, food arrived, cards arrived. Lots of phone calls from lots of friends. And I just muddled my way through it all. Sometimes paying attention, sometimes not. I think I thanked everyone, I hope so, but I'm really not sure.

And then all that stopped. The phone calls dribbled down to once or twice a week instead of daily, then even that stopped. And it's right that it stopped. While my friends cared about me and worried about me, they couldn't be expected to put their own lives on hold to take care of me.

So, out of desperation I sort of forced myself to wake up out of the daze of sadness that I was existing in. I looked around, and decided to stay alive. And, in order to do that, I had to figure out a way to keep living that involved something more than simply putting one foot in front of the other. I had to learn how to be alive all over again. And alive in a way that was entirely different than how I had been living for the last thirty years.

CHAPTER TWO

Sadness is a part of life for humans. We have lots of words for the emotion: sorrow, grief, bereavement, mourning, anguish, angst, misery, despair, suffering…and nothing really comes close to describing the feeling of loss. It's an emptiness of the soul, a place so deep and dark that before the thing happened that created the sadness, that place was unknown. A darkness that creeps in and envelops our entire being.

There it was, the empty darkness staring me in the face, surrounding me, threatening to overwhelm my life. Now I had to figure out how to not just deal with it, but live with it. And a decision had to be made: do I take to heart what so many of my well-meaning friends had told me about grief never going away and how I would have to learn to live with it? How I would have to make grief my new normal? Do I simply figure out some way to keep on existing with this emptiness, this overwhelming pain, or do I find a way to thrive despite everything? Is it possible to get to the point of being happy again? To wake up in the morning excited to live another day? And is that something I even wanted to do? It's so much easier to just exist, to go through the motions of living without really feeling alive all while still consumed with grief. But that isn't at all fulfilling and basic existence wouldn't fill up that empty place in my soul.

There is so much about grieving that involves guilt on so many levels. In my case, the most immediate and strongest guilt was because I hadn't been with Ben when he died and I felt, deeply felt that I should have been. I tormented myself with questions like: Was it essential for me to go home when I did? I could have stayed. "You should have stayed" my mind kept telling me. If I focused for very long on that, I would dissolve into tears and mentally beat myself up.

I felt guilty about all the times in the thirty years we were together that I got mad at him! I know that sounds silly and non-productive, and it is both. It's also real and part of the human condition. And, of course, I fixated on the last couple of months when he was in such bad shape both physically and mentally and needed so much help from me. I would dwell on how I was impatient because he couldn't remember how to get dressed and I had to help him figure out how to put his feet into his pant legs. Or how I had gotten angry because he stopped doing anything to help around the house...he was unable to do much of anything by that time, but I hadn't seen it that way and in my irritation at having to do everything myself I had decided that he was being lazy. And now he was dead and I was filled to the brim with guilt!

A minor thing made me realize how uncompromising I could be and had been: I had many nicknames for Ben ranging from Honey to Card Shark but a big one was Blanket-Thief. For years, when I made the bed in the morning, the blankets seemed to have always migrated over to his side, often leaving me freezing in the middle of the night. Yet somehow, I managed to always steal the top sheet. We laughed about this a lot over the years without either of us ever getting mad. But now Ben was gone and here I was making the bed in the morning and the blankets were still migrating over to Ben's side of the bed! Apparently, I had been pushing the blankets all along, he hadn't been stealing them. I ached to tell him about my discovery, we would have laughed so hard, but, of course, I couldn't tell him. You know what? I did anyway.

Feeling foolish but also kind of pleased with myself I stood in the bedroom and loudly said, "Honey, I don't know if you can hear me, and I feel like an idiot, but I want you to know that you are not a Blanket Thief! I'm a Blanket Pusher! I'm sorry I ever accused you of stealing our blankets." Then I cried.

So much guilt bubbled to the surface that I started to feel like I was a monster and I couldn't come to terms with the horrible person I was discovering that I was. To avoid facing up to the awful person I so obviously was, I hid in the fog of sorrow.

Friends called or sent flowers and cards. One dear friend, Alyssa, and her partner, Jen, left two big bags of goodies from Trader Joe's on my porch. Others tried their best to make sure I was all right. All of which was greatly appreciated. But none of this gave me a direction or mitigated the guilt.

One day I looked at my calendar and saw that two weeks had gone by since Ben died and I only remembered bits and pieces of that time. It was all foggy and disjointed.

I've always had an excellent memory and I was shocked to find that my memory had abandoned me.

Yet, somehow a seed had gotten itself planted in my mind. I don't know where that seed came from, but it was there. Possibly from the shock of being abandoned by my normally reliable memory. It was a tiny seed, but still a seed and that was the starting point to living again. Without my wanting it to, my mind had crawled out of its self-protective state of numbness and started to function. That night the seed took root and I had a sudden epiphany right in the middle of watching a stream of the series, "Castle." I sat straight up and let the thoughts erupt. And erupt they did at rapid speed.

Ben's health had started to get wonky about sixteen years before he died. Slowly at first and with periods, often quite long periods when he seemed to be just fine. Until then we had simply lived our lives together with all the hope and joy and love that married couples enjoy. And I tended to defer to Ben about most matters in our life…I think that's a generational thing.

But after that first health scare, I began to slowly take over our life together without even realizing it. I started making more and more decisions that impacted both of us and I told myself that I would only do that until Ben was back to one hundred percent then the reins would be all his again. Later, as I made even more decisions and did more and more of the things he had once done I told myself that it was so I could make sure that our life was running smoothly. Then, when his health got worse, I did all this just to see to it that Ben was well cared for. As his health started to really fall apart and dementia invaded his mind making life for both of us super difficult, I took over more and more until I was literally making every decision, and everything I did all day, every day was based solely on Ben and his needs.

And his needs kept getting bigger and bigger.

Finally, two years before he died, he took a nasty fall head-first down eight cement stairs. He scraped a lot of skin and hair off of his head, ripped up an arm and his back, and creamed both knees. He didn't break any bones and his head was intact and uninjured other than losing the skin and hair. But he never came back all the way from that fall. He had been sliding deeper into dementia for quite a while but it got much worse after this fall. Plus, he now had trouble walking and doing things like cutting up his food.

He was scared. And so was I.

That's when I took complete charge of our life. I made every decision. Every thought that I had was for Ben. Everything that I did was for Ben. I woke up every morning with one thought: Ben. What would his day be? What could I do to make his life better? What did he need me to do? What had I planned on doing for Ben? Without realizing it, I gave Ben one hundred percent of my life. One hundred percent of me.

There was nothing left over for Jill. My entire purpose, my only reason for living, my everything in life for more than two years had been Ben. And I don't regret one second of this. Not one! He needed me and I was there for him and I will always be glad of that.

But I lost myself in the process. Without Ben, I was empty and hollow and no longer had any reason to get up in the morning.

Mind you, I was blissfully unaware of any of this until that epiphany, and then it was an enormous shock. But I realized that if I was going to continue existing and maybe even discover a way to truly live and thrive, I had to find some kind of purpose that involved me…and I didn't know how.

It was right about then that I decided to seek the help of a grief counselor. I googled "grief counselors near me" and lots of sites came up, but they were confusing and overwhelming. So, I contacted our primary care physician and she referred me to a psychologist in her clinic. I tried to make an appointment with the clinic's scheduler and was told that the earliest that I could get would be the end of July. Since it was currently the end of May this simply wouldn't do. I begged for an earlier appointment and was told that perhaps I might be able to get on a waiting list and that someone would possibly call to maybe put me on that list the following Tuesday. It was then Thursday. Again, this would not do, and something lurking inside of me took over along with my acting training and I snarled, "Fine! I'll do my level best to not slash my wrists before next Tuesday! Thank you very much!" The scheduler quickly said, "Just a minute" and put me on hold. She came back in a couple of minutes and, wonder of wonders she had found an opening the following Monday.

The appointment, while somewhat helpful, was kind of a bust because the psychologist was a therapist, not a grief counselor. Grief counseling, I found out, is highly specialized and quite different than therapy. I spent the hour mostly answering questions about my childhood instead of talking about my grief. However, I think that session started me down a different road than the guilt-stricken road I had been stuck on. By pulling up many of the times that I had survived my difficult childhood, that hour showed me that I am a strong woman and even a kind one.

When I told the therapist about what I had done to get the earlier appointment she laughed and said that I was very inventive. The hour with that therapist made me realize that I can do whatever I truly decide to do since I had been doing exactly that my entire life without noticing it.

Of course, I still needed to figure out what I wanted to do with the rest of my life, but it was a start.

At the end of the session, the therapist said that I could have another appointment if I wanted and she gave me the phone number of a grief support group maintained by the clinic saying that I could certainly join that group if I wished. She also advised that most likely a support group would not be the best approach for either me or the group. She sort of intimated that I have a tendency to take over and that isn't the best approach in a support group. I suspect that I had taken over our session.

I chose to not join the group and not have another appointment with her at that time. Maybe in the future for actual therapy, but not for grief counseling.

Now the question became, what do I want to do with the years I have left? They didn't have to be empty years, either, now that I knew that I needed some kind of purpose. Only how do I find such a thing? How did other people find a purpose for their lives? To tell the truth, I had no idea. None. Zip. I was 81 years old, retired, on the edge of being broke, and alone. I had no family of my own, no children, no future as far as I could see. All of which, as you can imagine, was incredibly depressing.

And I missed my Ben more than I ever thought possible. If only I could have talked with him, given him my problem...he would have dealt with it using his dry humor and he would have come up with a way for me to move into the future. Not necessarily a way I liked, but a starting point. Sadly, he wasn't there and this was something that I had to do on my own. I can't tell you how much I hated that!

I discovered to my surprise that I could feel embarrassment. While in the market one day looking at artichokes, which Ben adored, I suddenly and without any warning burst into tears. The other shoppers stared at me and one nice woman asked if I was all right. I mumbled something like No, left my cart, ran out to my car, and just sat and cried.

That was awful, but it triggered the realization that I was alive and could feel something other than guilt and emptiness. I hugged that embarrassment to myself knowing, for the first time, that I was going to survive this. And I wanted to.

That was huge.

CHAPTER THREE

While one part of the world seemed to want to help and to be there for me; my friends and Ben's family, the rest of the world almost seemed as though it was conspiring to make life as difficult as it possibly could.

I had sent out one email to all the people we worked with that knew Ben, and phoned his family and closest friends. I hadn't thought about the rest of the world. In my sorrow and my naivety, I thought that the rest of the world would be considerate of someone who had just lost everything that counted in her life. I was so wrong.

The paperwork starts almost immediately and it continues for months. I understand that in some cases, where there are wills to probate and feuding family members, it can continue for years. For me, it was relatively simple…Ben didn't have a will and very little in the way of an estate, and still the whole process was gut-wrenching.

It started late on the night that he died.

Ben and I have both been very determined to leave our bodies to science. Basically, to leave our bodies to the med school where we had worked for so long. Ben had taught guitar in his youth, and later when working as a Standardized Patient he taught med students the proper way to take a blood pressure or do a correct heart-valve exam and many other procedures, so teaching was in his DNA. We had often talked about donating our bodies...Ben wanted to continue teaching after he died. But we...me...hadn't filled out the paperwork because, heck, there was still so much time ahead of us.

Until there wasn't.

So that's what I was doing when Ben died, getting witnesses to sign the forms so that his body could be donated to the med school.

The third phone call from the hospital/med school that night was brief and to the point. I was to come to the main reception desk the next morning to retrieve Ben's personal belongings. I could also give them the paperwork for his body donation at that time.

That was the first of many, many pieces of paperwork that needed to be attended to. I started getting emails requesting various things: "Please fill out the attached and return it by email." I had to supply information for his death certificate. That was especially hard for me. There was insurance to deal with. Social Security was something of a nightmare. I was put on hold and forced to listen to horrible "music" for hours on end. I'm still figuring out what needs to be done with the insurance.

I discovered that I had to notify all sorts of people and organizations. And every single time I did, I fell apart immediately after. And a lot of this happened during those first two brainfoggy weeks. I still don't know how much I got wrong but I suspect quite a lot.

I told the manager of our apartment complex almost a month after Ben died and found out that I had to bring him the death certificate so he could make a copy. I didn't have the death certificate yet, so that had to wait.

Social Security needed our marriage certificate which I didn't have. I had to get that from California and it took nearly 6 weeks. And I had to have a telephone meeting with someone from Social Security to answer questions. So many things that needed some other thing to be made right. And all this while I could barely function at all.

And more stuff that needs attention just seems to keep showing up. As I write this, I still have to notify the Screen Actors Guild and the Musician's Union as well as the utility companies and I have to take his name off of our credit cards. And every bit of doing these things makes his death so very final all over again.

These are things that I never gave a single thought to before Ben died. But every single one of them was and is painful. Every time I hear a stranger say the rote platitude, "I'm so sorry for your loss" I could scream! Instead, I just say "thank you" and try to ignore it.

All of these very important "have-tos" made life even more difficult and deepened my grief until at one point I truly didn't think I could go on. I wasn't sure I even wanted to.

CHAPTER FOUR

I have a weird quirk that I suspect I share with most people; songs invade my mind uninvited and bounce around in there sometimes for several days. I usually know only one or two lines of the song and repeating them over and over is maddening. Ben and I used to laugh about this. I would say, "You'll never guess what's playing in Jilly's head today." Then I would warble the two or three lines that I actually knew and the musician in Ben would groan and pretend that my off-key singing was super painful. Which, I have to admit, it is.

Usually, the songs that landed inside my head were the folk songs we both loved or the hits of the 1960s and 1970s. Maybe an old show tune. I would blast out the Sound of Silence or Greensleeves. Or maybe part of a song from Carousel or Oklahoma. Sometimes just the tune because I didn't know the lyrics and Ben would look unhappy and say that he couldn't tell what I was trying unsuccessfully to sing.

But the songs that showed up now were different and unnerving. The first one was "Honey" by Bobby Goldsboro, one of the maudlin songs of the late 1960s. Although it was never a favorite of mine, for some reason that I'll never understand, I knew more than just a couple of lines. The lyric that took over my brain was:

"See the tree, how big it's grown
But friend it hasn't been too long

It wasn't big.
I laughed at her and she got mad
The first day that she planted it
Was just a twig.

I came home unexpectedly
And found her crying needlessly
In the middle of the day.
And she was home and all alone
When the angels came
And took her away.

Now all I have is memories of Honey
And I wake up in the middle of the night
And call her name.
And now my life's an empty stage…"

These lyrics are considerably wrong, but that's what I had pounding away in my brain. And they made me cry. Every single time that they showed up. And I couldn't get the damn song out of my mind. For several weeks. And it still shows up every once in a while. And it still makes me cry, although now my tears are more gentle and not as wildly uncontrollable as they were then.

The next song that plagued me was "Ode to Billie Joe" by Bobbie Gentry. This had been a huge hit back in 1967 and people debated back and forth about what on earth had made Billie Joe MacAlister jump off the Tallahatchie bridge. But the only lyric that lived in my mind was:

"There was a virus going round
Papa caught it and he died Last Spring.
Now Mama doesn't seem to want
To do much of anything."

That perfectly described me...I didn't want to do much of anything these days. Not even things that I loved doing.

For some reason having this snippet of song rattling around in my brain gave me permission to not do anything. So, I didn't. I spent my days doing nothing more than the absolute bare minimum that had to be done. Feed the cats, heat up some mac & cheese, get the mail, pay a bill or two...that was about all I could handle.

Facebook is a marvelous distraction and I spent several hours a day distracting myself with memes of kittens and puppies. I found a page that featured lions and a man who lives with them in South Africa and hid in that for a while.

I discovered that I could still laugh because some of the memes are just plain over-the-top silly and laughing felt good. It also made me feel guilty again.

Many of the memes I wanted to share with Ben but, of course, couldn't. Sometimes I did anyway and would say aloud, "Look, honey! This is wonderful. You'll love it." Then I would feel like a complete fool. And utterly bereft.

I didn't post anything on Facebook about my husband dying, I'm not sure why other than I'm a fairly private person. I know it doesn't seem like it with this book, but usually I am extremely private. However, I think that Facebook, with all of its problems, helped me get through those first frightening days by simply giving me something else to think about. Something cute or beautiful or funny. Even for just a few minutes.

Still the darkness was always there. The emptiness. The feeling that I just didn't want to keep going on. I suspect that if I hadn't had the cats to take care of, I might have even joined Ben. And today the very thought of that leaves me more terrified than anything else I can think of.

Jill D'Aubery

Photo by Pam Helling

Ben and I discuss the meaning
of life with Winnie the horse

MY PATH TO JOY

CHAPTER FIVE

About two weeks after Ben died, my dear friend, Cindy, who has had her own share of heartbreak and understands it pretty well, sent me a self-care package. It was stuffed with all sorts of things to make me physically feel better. Face creams, an exfoliator, an overnight mask, hand rejuvenator, and a lovely little book called, "How to Survive the Loss of a Love" by Melba Colgrove, Harold H. Bloomfield, and Peter McWilliams.

This was a kind and gentle nudge for me to take some care of myself, which I hadn't been doing at all. Cindy is a film director and screenwriter and a student of the human condition and she recognized, as I did not, that the first thing we tend to do when living through such a loss is to stop taking care of ourselves. And to feel guilty if we do take care of ourselves.

About the only thing I had done to take any kind of personal care of my body was to brush my teeth. And I was completely unaware of how much I had let myself go until Cindy's gift arrived.

My first thought when I opened the box was what a sweet and lovely thing she had done. My next thought was, "Oh, my God! When did I last wash my face? Have I washed my hair recently? Or showered? Yikes! I must stink to high heaven." So, armed with the goodies in Cindy's box I marched into the bathroom and confronted a shockingly disheveled me.

I showered, washed my hair, and used as many of those goodies as I could. And, for the first time since Ben died, I almost felt human. At least I felt. And felt something besides sorrow and anger.

And that started me back on the road to living.

After that, I remembered my former habits of hygiene and self-care and began to take care of myself again. It took almost another week before I could look in the mirror and see something that wasn't scary and that almost resembled my old self. And a few days more before I truly gave a damn about how I looked. And I've always had a healthy streak of vanity!

Thanks to Cindy I cared about my physical self again and I will always be grateful to her for that.

I couldn't bear to open the book that she sent, but I left it out on the dining room table where I could see it every day. Somehow, the thought of reading about the loss of a loved one made my own loss feel even more real and more devastating. Until I opened that book, I could still play mind games with myself and I didn't have to accept his death. Not completely anyway.

I could postpone acknowledging that he was really and truly gone. If I worked at it, I could postpone it indefinitely.

Eventually, I did find the strength to open the book. I read it a couple of months after I got it and found it very helpful. It was filled with short admonitions about taking care of yourself and not blaming yourself and how it's okay to basically fall apart for a while. This was all very helpful and comforting to me. But it didn't end my grief. Instead, the book made it okay to grieve. And that is a good first step.

I thanked her by Facebook Private Messaging and she answered with the name and phone number of her cousin who had lost her husband suddenly about ten years ago and maybe could help me. I wasn't ready yet to talk to someone I didn't know about all this but I told Cindy that at some point I would make that call.

I still haven't made that call and I most likely won't. No real reason other than it simply doesn't feel right and these days I'm trusting my feelings more than I ever have before.

I did, however, reach out to another dear old friend, Bob. Bob and I hung out together and had lots of fun adventures back in our wayward youth, long before either one of us married, but I hadn't seen him in probably forty years. He had found me on Facebook some four or five years before and we chuckled over the FB antics of kittens and Walmart shoppers every once in a while. And back when Bob and I first reconnected, I told Ben about my old friend and we both decided that they would like each other very much.

I knew that Bob had lost his wife some fifteen years before and I thought that he might be able to help me navigate the ins and outs of grieving. But I didn't want to open any of his own wounds, so I tried to be as matter-of-fact and grown up as possible. That lasted for maybe one email. I may be 81 years old, but I'm hardly a grown up.

Bob was wonderful and helpful. He has managed to remain himself through his loss and I found myself emailing back and forth with a man who still had humor and was still the same caring person that I remembered. And before you think, Ah ha! Here comes the new romance...no, that isn't happening. Neither one of us is interested in romance, just in helping an old friend through an extremely difficult time.

Bob's first message after I contacted him was to tell me that I shouldn't expect any wisdom from him, that the shrink he had talked with hadn't helped much...and I could relate to that! And that I should take care to eat well and stay hydrated. Such practical advice. And such needed advice.

I realized that since Ben died, almost a month before, I had eaten almost nothing except mac & cheese. The kind that comes already made and just needs to be zapped in the microwave. And I had only been drinking water when I felt very thirsty. Maybe a couple of glasses a day, if that.

I charged into the kitchen and checked to see what I had in the fridge. It was pretty full and the first thing I saw was a package of steaks. That pleased me and I decided to cook one of them for dinner. But when I opened the package, the smell hit me and so did the green tint on the meat. Then I remembered that I had bought them when Ben went into the hospital so I would have them for his homecoming. They were over a month old and had gone bad.

I stood there in the kitchen holding the rotten meat and simply fell apart. The bad meat, a realization that I had eaten basically crap for a month, and that it had been almost a month exactly since Ben had died all hit me at the same time.

It was overwhelming and I just dissolved into grief.

Once I had cried myself out, I wiped my eyes and tossed the steaks. Then, having almost no energy left to figure out what to cook let alone to actually cook anything, it was back to mac & cheese for the next few dinners.

But lurking in the back of my mind was Bob's telling me to eat well, so that became the next thing that I did to try to recover. I went to the market and tried to find something easy yet nourishing.

I had been buying only cat food and mac & cheese for over a month and had no idea about what to get. Ben had been a marvelous audience for my cooking and I had trouble figuring out what to cook without that audience. Eventually, I settled on some salmon. Ben hated salmon and I like it, but hadn't cooked it in over thirty years so that seemed like a good idea. And it was.

That salmon opened my taste buds and my mind to the idea of eating for pleasure again instead of simply filling the empty hole.

That was the start of finding a path to joy in my grief.

CHAPTER SIX

Three days after Ben died, there was a horrendous school shooting in Uvalde, Texas and nineteen children plus two teachers were killed. And the war in Ukraine had been going on for months. Every news program on television was filled with both of these events every night for weeks and months. I watched parents with tears running down their cheeks, barely able to speak as they asked the impossible question: why was my child killed? My heart broke as I heard about the husband of one of the murdered teachers and how he had a heart attack and died himself three days after his wife was killed. He literally died of a broken heart.

I saw the faces of little children being put on a train and taken out of Ukraine, their stricken looks because at their young age they knew they may never again see their fathers. Their fathers who were staying behind to fight. I saw an old woman sitting outside the bombed out remains of her apartment building, her head in her hands as she cried for her dog that had died saving her.

Everywhere I looked I saw nothing but sadness and despair and that made my own sadness even deeper. But it also gave me yet another reason to feel guilty. After all, those parents, that husband, the people fleeing their homes

43

they all had experienced horrors much worse than my husband's quiet and peaceful death.

So, I tried to force myself to get it together. "Come on, Jill," I told myself. "These people are going through much worse than you are. What right do you have to suffer so much? They are really suffering, so knock it off! Pull yourself together and stop feeling sorry for yourself. Stop crying!" And then I would simply fall apart and sob. I was not only attempting to ignore my heartache, but I was also comparing my emotions to the emotions of people I didn't know, and that is a surefire road to misery.

There is another side to this coin.

Ever notice how some people are just happy souls? They can laugh at the most difficult things and have a gift for making other people laugh along with them. I'm not one of those people. Emotionally, I guess you could say that I'm fairly neutral. Although I'm empathic to a degree, the emotions that I feel from other people and mostly from animals are usually of the sad or desperate kind. I've always envied the naturally happy people, those folks who are able to find happiness wherever they go. And it never really occurred to me that even they have to work at it sometimes.

My friend, Jennifer, is one of those happy people. She always wears a big smile and is ready to laugh at just about everything. She does stand-up comedy; her persona is bigger than life and her booming voice can cut through almost anyone's sadness and plant a seed of delight smack in the middle of despair. So, it was shocking when I found her in tears at work a few years ago. I hugged her, which was all I could do to help, and she got through it and was back to her usual self in less than a day. Much later, when cancer hit her, she responded by laughing at it. At least that's how she responded in public. I have no idea about how she handled it privately. She defeated cancer, twice, and remained the bigger than life, funny, delightfully loud and very human Jennifer that I know and love.

I admire Jennifer, but I could never be like her. It's just not me. But remembering her tears and thinking about how she handled cancer made me realize that what people show the world is not necessarily what's going on inside of them. Jen's tears were real and so was the cause of them. Her cancer was real, so was the chemo that she endured. I haven't talked with her about her ordeal but I suspect that in the quiet times when she was alone, she grieved and felt every bit of the despair that she refused to show the world.

I also know that her laughter and her joyful approach to living is very real. Somehow, way deep inside of her, there exists a bottomless pool of delight at living. And she can call on that whenever she needs to, trusting that it will never fail her.

I thought about Jennifer as I looked at Ben's empty chair. I thought about how strong she is and how she magically manages to turn the awful into the wonderful. And I cried some more wishing I could find some way to do that. I suspect that Jennifer was born with this gift and she has honed it through life's difficulties until it became a shining beacon for her and for everyone around her.

Thinking about Uvalde and Ukraine filled me with guilt, as if I needed any more reasons to feel guilty. Then thinking about Jennifer and how different we are from each other made me begin to do something important about my own grief. It made me stop comparing myself, my life, my sorrow, and the way I was dealing with these emotions to anyone else. I could feel deep sadness for the people of Uvalde and Ukraine without feeling that my own grief was somehow unworthy. And I could envy Jen and her love of life without beating myself up for not being like her. I can be myself and feel however I happen to feel at any given moment. And that's okay.

It's also nobody's business but mine…I don't have to be either desperately sad or bravely cheerful in order to satisfy someone else's concept of how I should be handling my grief.

CHAPTER SEVEN

Ben had been gone for almost a month when I got a phone call from my friend, Pam. Another friend of ours, Trish, who had recently discovered a passion for making pottery, was having a sale of her creations and Pam had decided that she and I should go to this sale. I really didn't want to go but Pam insisted. And Pam is like a hurricane when she makes up her mind about something. She picked me up the day of the sale and was resolutely cheerful the entire day. Pam is a cheerful sort anyway, but that day she outdid herself.

Trish and her husband, Harold, and Pam all knew and worked with Ben and I think they were doing their level best to bring me out of the closed-off way I had been living since he died. I hadn't left our apartment except to go to the market and I suspect that I was, at best, distantly polite with friends on the phone.

The pottery sale was held at the studio where Trish did her work and, while the sale was inside there were some huge garage-type doors that were open so there was lots of ventilation. I was vaccinated and double boosted and I had been careful for over two years about masking which had pretty much become a habit. But with all that ventilation and a fairly sparse crowd I decided that it would be safe to take my mask off and breathe easily for a change.

Another friend, Lea, came by with delicious homemade brownies, and everyone was very kind and wanted to know how I was doing and sympathized with me about Ben. It was a nice afternoon, one that I greatly enjoyed much to my surprise since I hadn't really enjoyed much of anything for the past month. Even so I was more than ready to go home when it was over.

When Ben died and I found myself completely on my own, I discovered that I have a fairly strong streak of introvert that I never knew was there before. As yet I'm unsure of just how to be an introvert since I've always thought I was an extrovert, but I'm learning. Short bursts of socializing suit me just fine these days. I may at some point return to my former extrovert ways, I don't know. But for now, I'm content mostly being quietly alone.

A couple of days after the pottery sale I read on Trish's Facebook page that the very next day after the sale Harold had come down with covid and was now isolating. And I quietly freaked out. I had some home tests handy and tested myself right away. It was negative. I heaved a huge sigh of relief.

That was when I first realized that, yes, I did want to continue living, even without Ben. I still hadn't found a reason to live or a purpose to fill my days, but I wasn't ready to cash it all in just yet.

I was alive and wanted to stay that way.

CHAPTER EIGHT

On television the knottiest most complicated problems are solved in one hour. Intricate murders and involved romances that seem unsolvable are figured out in that hour. Every once in awhile it takes two hours, but that's about it. I think we tend to think that that is how life is. Or should be. We've been trained to expect a satisfying end to almost everything to occur in one hour or less. But life isn't that neat. Life is messy at best. And life doesn't always have a happy ending. In fact, at some point life will inevitably serve up a nasty jolt and leave us brokenhearted or angry or miserable.

And sometimes life does us a favor with that unpleasant jolt.

The day Ben died and I got that horrible phone call telling me of his death followed by the warm and caring phone call from the nurse, my emotions were all over the place. I didn't know what to do, how to react, what to say, who to call, and most of all, I didn't know how to ask for or get any help. So, I basically didn't do much of anything that might have helped me get through the grief.

The phone call from the nurse had pointed out to me how really awful the call from the Resident doctor had been.

The contrast was enormous and it made me angry. At the time I didn't realize that my anger was a good thing, I just knew I was furious. But that anger gave me something to do and, although I didn't know it then, it started me on the path to finding myself. Or at least to realizing that there just might be a path in the first place. And a self to find.

I reacted to my anger by firing off a couple of emails to some people Ben and I had worked with at the teaching hospital where Ben had died. Emails about the horrible way I had been told of Ben's death.

Ben and I had worked as Standardized Patients and later as Standardized Patient Trainers for thirty years. A SP is someone acting the part of a patient so that med students can practice dealing with "patients" before they do it for real. They can learn how to ask certain questions, what questions they need to ask, and perform basic physical exams without scaring or hurting a real patient. Simulation, as it's called, has become a very important part of all med schools in the U.S. and in most other countries as well. Passing a series of SP encounters is even required now for a doctor to be licensed to practice medicine in the U.S.

As you may imagine SPs portray patients with pretty much every known disease or physical problem you can think of, and a person working as an SP for very long will acquire a fairly decent working knowledge of medicine just by absorption. Ben and I used to joke that we were probably right around the level of a Third-Year med student and knew just enough about medicine to thoroughly annoy our own doctors but not enough to actually know what we were talking about.

I had spent the past ten years or so writing scripts for the various scenarios in the Sim program and I had to work closely with faculty to make sure the scripts were accurate and yet made sense to the actors. So, I had gotten to know most of the faculty pretty well.

I was so angry about that phone call from a clueless Resident that I decided to do something about it. With my anger still raging I fired off an email to a woman I had worked with who runs the Ethics Dept. at the med school describing the phone call and my anger. I told her that I knew the med students at our school did receive some training in how to give bad news, but I also knew that Residents come from all over the country, and even from other countries and that we have no idea about any training that they may or may not have received about giving bad news. I said that Residents coming into our school should receive training, extensive training, about how to deliver bad or scary news and that they should get this training right at the start of their time at our hospital/university. Way before they have a chance to do a terrible job of giving such news.

I hit "Send" and forgot about it. My anger had been dealt with and I slipped back into the fog of sorrow.

To my great surprise, Susan emailed me back and said how sorry she was to hear about Ben and she asked if it would be all right if another person from the Ethics Department would contact me to talk about my experience. It turned out that she was, herself, going through something similar and had taken a leave from work. I emailed back, Yes, and forgot about it again as I jumped back into my safe fog.

It took a little while, things never move quickly in large organizations, but I was contacted by Amanda also of the Ethics Dept. It was a good thing that it took some time because she contacted me shortly after that big epiphany and while I was trying to find some kind of purpose that could carry me forward. Amanda provided that purpose. At least she provided the initial, immediate purpose, and one that jolted me out of the lethargy that I had been living in.

It's often said that God, if you're religious, or the Universe if you are not, sometimes has to give you a strong whack up the side of your head with a 2x4 to get your attention. And that is exactly what happened with Amanda. Of course, she had no idea that she was wielding a 2x4, but she was and I'm glad of it.

Amanda's email said that she wanted to come over to my apartment with a videographer and tape an interview with me about the way I was told about Ben's death. This was a very good thing and even more than I had ever hoped would happen in response to the angry email I had sent to the Ethics Dept.

But my initial reaction was total panic. Very human panic. And that panic eventually pushed me into tiptoeing out of the fog and venturing into the sunshine. Mind you, I did not much care for the sunshine, the fog was certainly easier and way more comfortable plus I had gotten used to living in fog. But that was not to be for very much longer.

Amanda's email asked if a date roughly two weeks in the future would work for me. I looked around my apartment and with newly if temporarily fog-removed eyes saw the frightful mess I had allowed it to become. About the only thing I had bothered to do for well over a month was to wash the dishes, and I had only done that because I needed to have something to eat the mac & cheese on.

Two weeks! I had two weeks to get the apartment into some kind of reasonable shape.

Okay, I thought. *I can do that.*

Still, I made one rather feeble attempt to avoid having to clean up the mess by suggesting to Amanda that I was up for pretty much any venue she wanted and that my apartment was small and not very interesting. My actual words were, "My apartment is sort of small and has been decorated by that famous French firm, Les Feline, so if there's another place that you would like to use to film, that would be fine with me."

However, she wrote back, "I've heard that Les Feline is ever so chic and trendy and does fantastic work, and it would be lovely to capture you in your own habitat if you're open to that!"

She completely won me over with her comment about Les Feline. So, feeling trapped I agreed to the date and to taping in my apartment...and cleaning it. Including the cat-shredded furniture.

And since then, I have blessed this lovely lady many, many times!

I have to say here that I'm a Libra and my Libran motto is, "Never put off until tomorrow what you can just as easily put off until next week." So, typical of me even on good days, I put off the bulk of the cleaning. But I did attack the scary bathrooms.

I was right in the middle of scrubbing Ben's tub when, with no warning at all, I suddenly burst into song. And not the maudlin songs that had been living in my head.

No, I found myself singing The *Jet Song* from West Side Story!

"When you're a Jet
You're a Jet all the way
From your first cigarette
To your last dying day.

When you're a Jet
If the spit hits the fan
You've got brothers around
You're a family man!"

And I followed that with, *Cool*, also from West Side Story.

"Boy, boy, crazy boy!
Get cool boy.
Got a rocket
In your pocket
Stay coolly cool boy."

And I liked singing these songs, even badly. Which made me realize that I was feeling something that felt good for a change. And I enjoyed the feeling. Imagine that…I was enjoying something!

That really was the start of coming back. Of coming out of the all-encompassing fog of misery. I had crept out of the fog a few times, but not for very long and I hadn't liked it so I had dived back into the safety of being enveloped by a mental haze as fast as I could. And I didn't even know that I was doing that.

This time, cleanser in one hand and scrubbing sponge in the other, I belted out as much of West Side Story as I could remember.

And the fog lifted completely and was gone. Forever. It has never come back. My focus had changed from how miserable I was to how wonderful the music of West Side Story is.

I've never seen West Side on stage and I had only seen the original movie once, way back in 1961 when it first came out. I still hadn't seen Steven Spielberg's new version and I found myself curious about the differences that I had heard about.

And there I was, thinking about something other than how much I missed Ben! I had poked my head up out of my sorrow, looked around, and discovered that there is life out there.

And life was calling to me.

So, I checked and discovered that the two films were available to me from Comcast and I decided to watch them both.

This was such a small thing really, but such a huge thing for me at that time because it was the first thing that didn't revolve around Ben and how sad I was. I was finally interested in something outside of myself.

That night I made some real food and some popcorn, settled myself in front of the TV, and watched Spielberg's version of West Side Story, then later that night I went on Facebook and wrote a little review of it. The next night I watched the original movie, also with some real food and popcorn. And again, went on Facebook and wrote a review that compared the two versions.

And for the first time since Ben died, and really for quite a long time before he died, I felt like Jill. And like Jill mattered and had interests beyond either herself or her sorrow.

When you think about it, it's really kind of strange that West Side Story of all things would bring me out of myself when the entire premise of the play is all about love that is lost to death. I think it was the music. That music is so vital and pulsing and alive, it simply refuses to be denied.

This isn't to say that I was suddenly just fine…I wasn't. But I had been jolted out of my complacent, comfortable, and by then normal-feeling misery. Now I could look around me and think of something other than how sad and empty I was. The sadness was still there, but I wasn't lost in it anymore.

The fog did not come back. I was aware of myself and my surroundings again. And I almost liked that. Almost.

CHAPTER NINE

Armed with my newfound awareness, I faced the coming taping with a sense of excitement and even a bit of purpose. I attacked my messy apartment with some sort of vengeance; however, I did concentrate on the parts that I figured Amanda and the videographer, Corky, would primarily be in. And, of course, I was wrong. They managed to roam all over the place including the still-messy parts. But they didn't seem bothered by that, so I decided to not be bothered either.

Well prepared, Amanda arrived with a long list of questions that she planned to ask during the interview, but the first question pretty much set the tone. It was a simple question, one that all doctors should ask of someone who is grieving, one which no one had asked me up until that time…and my answer did what it was supposed to do. It reached inside and opened up my heart and poured sunshine into it.

The lighting was set up and a microphone was attached. The sound levels were taken and we were ready to go. Amanda asked her first question, "So, tell me a little bit about Ben. What was he like?"

And there it was. The question that for years I'd been telling med students that they need to ask, the question I had forgotten about, and that question was now being asked of me.

When you live with someone you don't really think about the overall picture of who they are or what they're like. It's more the day-to-day stuff. The things that make you proud or angry or happy or sad are fleeting yet they are part of the mosaic that makes a person who they are. Bits and pieces of the whole person so to speak.

I have no idea what I said, but I know I went on and on about Ben. I think I talked about how he was a musician and an actor. Maybe about how he loved puzzles and word games. A little something about his love of animals and cats in particular. I may have left out the part about how when we first started dating he considered squirrels to be just rodents, awful little rats with fluffy tails, and how he changed that idea once he got to know some squirrels and how he wound up liking them. I adore squirrels and made sure that he met a few of them along the way.

So, my Ben had an open mind and was willing to change a long-held idea if he got new information. I think that made him a remarkable man.

And that's the kind of thing I talked about.

The taping went on for quite a while. Amanda asked a couple more questions but mostly I just talked. And talked. And talked. I don't know what I said, but Amanda was happy and at one point I looked up at Corky and saw tears on his cheeks. I cried several times and laughed a couple of times. I know I talked about how Ben and I met and that it took thirty-three years and a few bad marriages for each of us before we got together for real. And how it took Ben eight long, long years to get around to proposing. I'm pretty sure that I talked about how we were seldom apart in the thirty years we were together…how we lived, worked, played, and did everything together. We were closer than bark on a tree. And we liked it that way.

When Amanda and Corky left and I was alone again I felt different. At least I felt different than I had felt in, I don't know how long. I didn't recognize this odd feeling for a few hours, then suddenly it hit me! I felt good! I felt whole! I felt not just like myself but like a happy myself!

And naturally almost as soon as I recognized this, I felt ashamed for feeling happy! We humans are strange creatures at best.

That was, as I write this, about a month ago and since then I've done a lot of thinking about that day. The guilt that came after the taping was surprising since it came right on top of the strange feeling of being happy. And it's taken until now for me to figure it out. And I haven't figured out the two conflicting emotions completely, but enough to deal with them.

First the sudden, unexpected feeling of happiness. Just talking about Ben, who he was, what he loved, how brave and strong he was, and the funny, weird person that he could be opened up a floodgate of memories. Good memories. And when good memories surround and fill us, our minds remember and feel all that joy and goodness again regardless of what else is going on. (Physically, I suspect this involves endorphins being released in our brain by pleasant emotions. Endorphins are hormones that help relieve pain, reduce stress, and improve our sense of well-being.)

I talked about us, our life together, the good times and the not-so-good times, and I cried both happy tears and sad ones. But my emotions and my feelings about Ben were no longer bottled up inside with no way out. My love for Ben, and his love for me, was right there, out in the open, exposed for all the world to see.

And the last several years of stress and fear melted away. The memories that I would carry forward into the rest of my life would now be the joyful memories of our happy, wonderful, sometimes scary, always loving life together.

If I may be so bold as to recommend a way forward to those who are filled with grief it would be this: Sit down with a trusted friend or relative and a videotaping camera, or just the camera if you prefer, and talk about the loved one that is gone. Talk openly and honestly about your memories. Let it all hang out, as we used to say. Cry and laugh and don't give any thoughts at all to what anyone else might think. This is about you and your beloved and only you and your beloved. You are the only person in the entire world who has experienced this life of yours, so you get to talk about it for as long as you want and in as great a detail as you want. I would say write it all down, but it seems that speaking it, and using your voice seems to make a huge difference. At least it did for me.

As time goes along and sadness creeps back into your soul, and it will, pull out that video and watch it. And let the memories wash over you all over again. It might make you miss your love even more, but it will also give you the ammunition you need to support the joy you had in your life with your beloved. And the strength to move forward with joy into your life as it is now.

For me, following that remarkable feeling of happiness, there was the inevitable guilt. For a change, this particular guilt was fairly easy to deal with since it was pretty darned easy to figure out. I felt guilty because I had thoroughly enjoyed making that video and what right did I have to enjoy talking about my husband who was dead and could not share that enjoyment with me? What right did I have to feel good or happy without him? Even for a couple of minutes.

Logically, of course, I had every right in the world to feel whatever way I felt with or without Ben. But logic has a funny way of escaping through that back door when emotions are involved. So, relying on logic didn't work. I still felt guilty.

And now my emotions were more than a little confusing. On one hand, I was happy and excited about the video because it was going to be used to help people. On the other hand, I was once again consumed with guilt about feeling happy and excited.

So, I decided to do something truly weird about the guilt. First of all, I asked myself what I wanted for the rest of my life. Did I want to feel good or did I want the guilt to continue? That was easy, while I still felt guilty about possibly being able to feel good, I made the decision that I wanted to feel good. Okay, then. Feeling good was certainly an option. But could I feel good while I missed my Ben so much? Wishing I had Meryl Streep around to tell me how she reaches inside to find the right emotion to portray and how she knew which emotion was the right one, I tried searching through my memories. These memories turned out to be of others that I had lost in the past.

All of us lose those we love throughout our lives. And we react differently to each loss. I had lost my grandparents, my parents, and my brother, as well as many cats and a few friends by this time in my life. I finally settled on the loss of Springer, a tabby cat that had welcomed Ben to the family the first time they met. He had been a remarkable cat and a bit of a monster, but very loving and way too smart for his own good. He died when he was fifteen just a couple of months after Ben's second mom and his sister died. We had held ourselves together when Anne, Ben's sister, died and when Vy died a couple of months later, but when Springer died it was just too much and we both simply fell apart. We cried and cried and missed our boy so much that it physically hurt. Of course, we were also mourning the loss of Anne and Vy, but we focused our grief on Springer.

Anne had died young of lung cancer. Her death had been expected but it was still shocking. I think most of us somehow thought that she would manage to find her personal back door and escape the enviable. This was partly because she was so thoroughly enjoying her life when she found out about her cancer. It was nearly impossible for anyone who knew Anne to think that she could die when she was still so glamorous, so beautiful, and so filled with life.

Anne was only 56 when she departed our world leaving her two adult children, her brother, and her cousins behind. She also left a fairly large contingent of friends. And she had an impressive memorial filled with family and friends which achieved its purpose of closure and reassuring those left behind that their own lives would continue albeit without Anne.

Vy's death was different. For one thing, she was in her early 80s when she left us, and even though the death of someone at any age is heartbreaking, we can accept it more easily when the person who dies is old. Especially if they have lived a long and, hopefully, good life. Vy also had cancer and had fought it bravely. But when the end grew close her cancer manifested in several brain tumors which meant that she didn't die quickly or with ease, she went by inches. She phoned me one day, just a few weeks before her death, to tell me that she had lost the color blue and that she missed it. Then came other things she lost; speech became very difficult as did walking. Finally, about three weeks before she died, she fell into a coma.

When Vy left us we were all heartbroken, but although no one said it, we also knew that we had, in fact, lost her weeks before her actual death.

That was a hard Winter for the entire family, but we accepted our losses and continued on. As we had to do.

Then came Springer. An innocent little cat who depended on Ben and me for literally everything. Springer was a tough, adventurous cat. He liked people, other cats, dogs, pretty much everyone. He caught birds but brought them home unhurt…it was as though he wanted to be friends with them. He had found the love of his life a mere two years before he died and he and Patches were inseparable. The one thing he hated was trips to the vet, and getting him into the cat carrier for such a trip usually took a good hour, lots of patience, and more than a few band-aids.

So, when he started getting into the carrier on his own and yowling we knew something was wrong. Really wrong. It was as though he was asking us to take him to the vet. Which we did. We discovered that he had a large mass behind his left lung that was pressing on his heart and was inoperable. We had to make a decision right then and there.

He was quiet but never took his eyes off Ben and me. We made the awful decision to let him go…and that was so hard to do.

And he knew, that was the hardest part of all…he knew.

The vet gave him a shot to calm him before giving him the shot that would end his life, and he used the last bit of strength that he had to pull himself over to the edge of the exam table and put his head on my breast. He purred as he left us. I was crying. Ben was crying. The vet and her assistant were crying.

Over the years I've thought about why Springer's death hit us so much harder than Anne and Vy's had done. Ben and I talked about it a lot and finally figured out that we lived with Springer, we didn't live with either Anne or Vy. So, our desolation when we came home with an empty cat carrier was heavily felt. And everything was different for us without him.

Thinking about all this in my attempt to deal with the guilt I was experiencing about feeling reasonably good after making that video led me to understand that literally every single thing that happens to us changes us. Most in microscopically small ways, but others in profoundly big ways. The deaths of both Anne and Vy had changed us, we missed both women, but we had been living our lives without either of them making too great an impact on us other than we loved them and enjoyed spending time with them. We didn't live our daily lives with them.

But Springer had changed us greatly simply because he had had a daily impact on us for fifteen years. So, did I feel guilty about missing my cat so much? Or did I feel guilty because his death had a greater impact on me than the deaths of Anne and Vy? To tell the truth, I'm still working on that one.

The upshot of this rather long memory was that in the space of four months Ben and I had lost two very important people in our lives and one very important cat. And, looking back at that time, we had not "learned to live with the grief" but managed to remember the good times with each of them instead of focusing on our loss. We didn't decide to do this, we didn't even know we were doing it, but we did it. And by focusing on the funny, embarrassing, strange, awful, and wonderful times we had with them we found laughter and the joy that can come from remembering.

And that gave me the strength and the ability to let go of the guilt I was feeling now. And to not feel guilty about letting the guilt go!

CHAPTER TEN

My friend, Bob, emailed something that made me stop and think: "I remember that I didn't want to see friends because they would offer condolences and that was like reopening the wound. Not their fault, they were doing the right thing. I just couldn't handle it properly."

I had been avoiding my friends and wasn't even aware that I was doing this. I wasn't avoiding them like, "Go away! Leave me alone!" or anything, more like simply not being available to them. And just when they were doing their utmost to help me.

I read Bob's words again and they resonated with me. Strongly. And just reading them made me realize that while I was going through the deepest heartbreak I've ever had, and I was suffering and having trouble just getting through my days, my friends were trying to help me and I had closed them off.

And my closing them off certainly wasn't helping me in any way at all. They must have noticed my pulling back, but being good friends, they never said a word about that to me, they just kept on trying to help.

So, here was yet another layer of guilt for me to deal with! Yay!

This new guilt made me wonder if I even wanted to be helped. If I deserved to be helped. That question ricocheted around in my mind for days while I fielded various phone calls and turned down invitations for lunch so I could stay in my safe foggy numbness. Then a couple of days after reading those words from Bob I suddenly thought about how sad it was that he couldn't handle seeing his friends. Bob is a pretty gregarious guy and loves being around people and people also love being around him. So, his pulling back was extremely sad to me. And that made me face up to finally asking myself this question: Do I *want* to be helped? Do I *want* to feel better? Or do I want to stay in the fog?

I'm a bit of a strange duck…you may have noticed that already…but when I have something that I need to ask myself or deal with about myself I tend to do it in front of a mirror.

And that's what I did this time. I marched into the bathroom and confronted the mirror.

I was somewhat gratified that I no longer looked like death warmed over. Some basic taking care of myself by doing things like bathing and washing my hair plus eating some real food had worked wonders. So, feeling reasonably okay, I stood in front of the mirror and had a nice chat with myself.

"Here's the thing, Jill," I said, "your friends are knocking themselves out being there for you and you are doing your level best to ignore them. How come?"

I thought about what Bob had written and decided that that was exactly right. It seemed as though every time I managed to get to the point of looking ahead without too much fear of the future, some dear friend would tell me about how sad she was to hear about Ben. And it was just like ripping off the scab that had formed to protect a wound.

"Okay, so here we are," I said to Jill in the mirror. "You are sad, broken-hearted, in fact, but so are your friends. Yet they are doing everything they can for you, Jill. So, it comes down to this…do you want to be alone? Completely alone? Because that's what's coming, that's your future if you aren't able to be grateful to your friends for all the loving things that they're doing for you."

Of course, the tears flowed and the shame soared, but somewhere inside of myself I realized how much these friends meant to me…and apparently, I must have meant something to them as well.

I've always been a powerfully independent person, able to take care of myself, so it's hard for me to ask for help of any kind. Or to accept help from anyone. I thought back to the Oscar-worthy performance that I pulled off when I got the appointment with the grief counselor and had to chuckle. Have you ever chuckled while in the middle of crying? It's quite an experience!

I looked at my tear-streaked face and made a decision: I will not deny my friends their chance of being able to deal with Ben's death by being there for me. It's the least I can do for them. And at that time, it was also the most I could do for myself.

And that left me with a determination to be the friend to them that my friends were being to me.

Then came the guilt. "Maybe I deserve to be alone," I told the mirror. "Maybe I'm just not a good enough person to deserve anything except being alone." I studied my face for several minutes.

Then, for no reason that I could explain, a memory flooded my mind.

A woman that I worked with had had to say goodbye to her beloved dog and she was pretty torn up over it. I've lost so many pets, you do if you live for a long time, and I knew what she was going through. That night I sent her a copy of a wonderful little essay by Eugene O'Neil called, "The Last Will and Testament of a Very Distinguished Dog" and I warned her to read it in a few days after the initial shock had worn off a bit. I also suggested that she have a box of Kleenex handy when she did read it. A couple of weeks went by and then I got an email from her that said how much she appreciated the essay and how much it had helped her. So much, in fact, that she was now considering getting a puppy which she had vowed to never again do because it was just too hard when they left us.

So, I had been of some help to someone in the past. Maybe I wasn't such a clunky person after all. Maybe there was some worth to me. And maybe, just maybe I was worth caring about.

Maybe I was even good enough to let go of this one guilt at least.

And, strange as it seems, that particular guilt just sort of faded away right then and there. I could almost feel it leaving me.

I still had a huge assortment of guilts filling up my mind and my soul. But that particular guilt was gone. And I felt good about that. I even felt good about feeling good.

Imagine that! I felt good about feeling good. Surely I could scramble up yet another reason to feel guilty about feeling good, couldn't I?

I stared at myself for quite a while, waiting for the expected guilt to show up. But it didn't. So, after almost an hour of standing in front of the mirror and not feeling guilty, I washed my face, blew myself a kiss, and said, "Okay, old girl. Let's do this."

I called one of the friends I had been ignoring. "Hi. It's me. Just wanted to check in and see how you're doing. And to tell you how much I really appreciate all the phone calls you've been making to me."

That was such a big step. And such a good one.

CHAPTER ELEVEN

My mother died in 1968, my father in 1996, and my brother in 2013. And that was my entire family. I don't have any children and neither did Ben. So, other than friends and Ben's family, I am entirely alone. No aunts or uncles, no nieces or nephews, no one. Just me. And that's all right. In some strange and unpredictable ways, it's even a good thing.

All families are different, there isn't any rulebook about how families should be.

Families range from Leave it to Beaver and Father Knows Best to the interesting family in Dallas and even the Royals. But, different from each other as they are, it's still true that no one except someone in your family has the guts or the permission to say to you something like, "Whew! When was the last time you showered? You could stop a train with that stink! Get your butt in the shower now." No one but family knows you well enough to make sure you eat and eat well when the last thing you want to do is lift a fork. Family, close family, knows when you're lying no matter how well you do it, and they know when you're not taking care of yourself regardless of how loudly you

71

protest that you are taking excellent care of yourself. Family will help you with the mountain of bills that you just couldn't face and family will call for help when you couldn't possibly give a damn if you get help or not.

So, at the worst time in your life, your family is there for you. And when someone in your family is at the worst point in their life, you are there for them. It works out very well. You may not want your family's help, and you might resent their meddling, but ultimately, you'll be very grateful that they loved you enough to bully you into cleaning up your act and finding your footing again.

But all that loving help can also slow down the process.

Bob said something about how much his daughter had helped him. Especially in those first, early days. And it seems as though now, fifteen years later, she is still a great support for him. And I couldn't be happier that he has that. But it seems from his emails that he is still living in a bit of a fog and hasn't been able to get entirely past that horrible sadness.

He said something about how amazing I am because I am striving to find happiness and not stay forever in grief. He said that his goal is simply coping. And because he's Bob and has one of the best and driest senses of humor that I've ever known he tossed in, "I don't have to be happy and you can't make me!" as something he presumably thinks about his daughter's efforts.

And that started me thinking...always a dangerous thing for me to do. And this is what I came up with: Bob, and for that matter, most of my friends, had help from their families in dealing with their own grief. Someone was there to help them get through those first, frightening days. And someone is still there to make sure that they're okay.

I didn't have any kind of family help like that. I was completely on my own to deal with the grief of losing my Ben. My friends were great, they went out of their way to help, but they're not family. No matter how much they care, no matter how much they love me, not one of my friends could confront me on the important things of daily life. Nor should they. That's not their job. And they would probably feel icky if they tried.

So, because I am alone with no one that I've known my entire life who could drop by and say, "Oh boy! When did you last wash that bird's nest on your head? Here's some shampoo, off you go. Wash that thing!" No one made sure that I ate decently. No one forced me to continue doing my days. And no one is going to be there to make sure I'm okay a year from now or ten years from now. That's the job of family, and I have none.

I have to do all that family stuff myself. I'm the one who had to figure out that I needed to shower. I'm the one who had to force myself to eat and, eventually, eat something other than mac & cheese. I'm the one who had to look in the mirror and recoil from what I saw. I had to tell myself to shape up. There was no way I could pick my feet up and let someone else carry my load for a while as I slowly recovered. Not if I was going to do more than simply cope. Not if I was going to live.

And once I decided that I did want to live I took the next step and decided that I wanted to do more than just live...I wanted to thrive. And because I had to do it all myself, I did it. And just doing even the smallest thing that was exclusively for me, gave me some strength that I didn't know that I had and that made it possible to do the next thing. And the next. Until taking a shower, eating, laughing, and even cleaning something felt right and became normal.

My "new normal" isn't about grief, it's about really living and enjoying my life. Now I'm learning how to do that without feeling guilt-ridden about it.

CHAPTER TWELVE

I started college in summer school back in 1958. My major was Theatre Arts, but there were some other required subjects that I had to take and Psych 101 was one of them. This class was something of a joke since it was taught by the Basketball Coach and he seemed to be roughly one chapter ahead of us in the book. So, really, I know nothing about the subject. I have three friends who are practicing psychologists, but they've never practiced on me, nor should they. However, it will be interesting to hear what they have to say when they read this book.

Everything that I'm writing is strictly from my own point of view. This is what happened to me and how I handled it. I have no idea if psychologically I did it well or badly, all I know is how I feel today. And today I'm feeling pretty good. I suspect that the reason I managed to live with the death of my husband and all the sorrow and heartbreak that goes with that is because I was willing to make a decision. A decision that I just didn't want to live in pain for the rest of my life. And that meant that I had to find a way to deal with all the guilt that such a decision entails.

And, hoo boy, is there ever a ton of guilt!

And it started almost immediately with the awareness that I was alive and Ben was dead.

At first, I didn't know about the guilt, I just felt like total crap. I was in shock so crap and numbness were about all I was able to feel at that point. There was also some anger because of the horrible phone call that I had gotten telling me that Ben was dead, but mostly I just felt awful. I found and retreated into that safe, foggy place pretty quickly. In there I didn't have to feel anything, I could just exist and not think, not feel...until the phone rang or flowers were delivered. I poked my head out of the fog every once in a while, to thank someone for doing something nice for me, then as fast as I possibly could I jumped back into the fog.

Thinking back, I realize how shrouded in guilt and remorse I was, and how I was so bound and determined to stay that way.

Bob had said something in an email about how his daughter had insisted that he had to accept and get used to his "new normal" and he knew she was right but it still irritated him. I don't know if he ever asked his daughter exactly what this "new normal" was supposed to be. I hope he did, but I have a feeling that he didn't simply because that question never came up. I'm pretty sure that the reason her insistence irritated him is that the "new normal" he was living in at that point and simultaneously trying not to live in was more than a little uncomfortable. It probably felt like he was drowning in unresolved sorrow while putting on a pleasant face for the world to see.

Bob's email made me realize that I didn't want to accept and live in any "new normal" that involved being forever in the grip of sorrow. I didn't want my days to be about putting one foot in front of the other and hoping to not fall apart. I was coming out of the shock of losing my Ben, and the fog had retreated, hopefully forever, but I still needed to find something that would make my life worth living again. And whatever that was going to be, it had to be something that would not just hide the grief but would let me deal with it out in the open while not letting it take over my life.

But, to do that I had to deal with a ton of guilt. And since guilt is such a slippery chameleon and able to disguise itself in all manner of life's costumes, the first thing I had to do, right after deciding to find joy in my life, was to seek out the various guilts that had become a part of me.

When I started to actively look for the guilts that owned me, I found them and I was stunned at how much guilt there was lurking in my soul. I don't know if most people are like me in this respect, but I think I've managed to feel guilty about almost everything in my life! The stuff I dredged up was astonishing. And not just about Ben, either.

There was the time that my father took my brother and me to Knotts Berry Farm. I was probably seven and my brother was eleven. There is a large fountain at the farm, and people make a wish then throw coins into it. My father gave me a dime and lifted me up to stand on the rim while I made my wish and tossed my coin.

I was working on the wish, it had to be just right after all, when my father suddenly swooped me up in the air and I dropped my coin into the fountain without making a wish. And I was furious! I lashed out at him in a full-on seven-year-old rage and refused to speak to him for the rest of the day. The adult Jill was chagrined when I remembered this event and I wished I could apologize for my childish behavior and my temper. But I couldn't do that since my father was long dead. I apologized anyway, out loud to my father and also to myself.

There was a ton of stuff from my childhood, but I had lived with all of that my entire life, so dealing with that guilt, while probably a really good idea at some point, preferably with the help of a therapist, was something I could put off so I could concentrate on the guilts that revolved around Ben.

I'm not going to delve into all the stuff I found out, the important thing is that I chose to deal with it. Every bit of it. The big things and the small things. The biggest was that I had not been with him when he died, and the smallest, or at least the silliest, was the title of Blanket Thief I had saddled him with.

I had no idea of just how to go about this. When someone is in therapy on a TV show the therapist looks knowingly at the patient, cocks an eyebrow, and says something along the lines of, "And how did it make you feel when you saw little Johnny fall off his bike?" The patient looks confused for a couple of seconds, then has a lightbulb moment, and blurts out, "Oh, my God! I felt like the king of the hill!" And is thereafter a well person. But real life isn't at all like that. Ask any therapist!

So, I spent some time floundering and not knowing what I was doing, just that I had to do something. And finally, I took control. By this time, I was more than aware of most of the guilt I was living with, and almost everything I did during my days seemed to add more. And I knew that as long as I was submerged in all that yucky guilt, I would never be free. Just figuring that out was enormously helpful.

So, back to my friend, the mirror. My quirky mind pictured another whole dimension on the other side of that mirror with a large audience enjoying my misery…and my growth. In my mind, lots of "Other Dimensional Folks" were pulled up in big easy chairs watching me while drinking beer and munching on popcorn. All of which I must admit I kind of enjoyed.

I stood in front of the mirror and talked to myself. I asked myself the questions I fondly, and most likely incorrectly, thought a therapist might ask:

Therapist Jill: So, you've decided that you want to enjoy the rest of your life, right?

Plain Old Jill: Yes. Kind of. I guess.

TJ: You guess? You don't know?

POJ: No. I don't know. Not absolutely anyway.

TJ: Hmm. So, how are you feeling right now?

POJ: I don't know how I'm supposed to be feeling.

TJ: How do you want to feel?

POJ: *Tears starting.* Not like this.

TJ: So, what's stopping you?

POJ: *Gulps and shakes off the tears.* I have no idea.

TJ: Think about it. What's holding you back from enjoying your life?

POJ: I don't know. *Thinks for a second or two.* Maybe I'm just not good enough. *I couldn't save him. I wasn't good enough.*

TJ: Why is that?

POJ: I don't know! You tell me!

TJ: Could you be feeling guilty about something?

POJ: *Tears.* I couldn't save him! I wasn't good enough to save him!

TJ: Could anyone save him?

POJ: *Hesitantly, wiping tears away.* No.

TJ: So, how does that make you feel?

POJ: Angry. Helpless. Useless.

TJ: And how does that make you feel?

POJ: *Snarling.* This isn't a TV show, damn it!

TJ: Fine. Let me know when you're ready to talk about it.

POJ: *Taking a deep breath.* Damn you! *One more deep breath.* Okay. I'm ready. I think.

Other Dimensional Folks applaud.

TJ: *Silently cocks an eyebrow.*

POJ: *Launches into a long, tearful description of all the terrible things she did to her husband over the years. Omitting nothing, and feeling like a puddle of pure poo.*

TJ: Well done. Now how do you feel?

POJ: Like a terrible person. All those awful things I've done or thought.

TJ: Are you a terrible person? Or just a human person who isn't perfect?

POJ: *A couple of tears slide down her cheeks.* I guess I'm just kind of human. Is it all right to be imperfect and wrong so much?

TJ: What do you think?

POJ: *Wiping the tears away.* I guess it makes me me.

TJ: Do you like you?

POJ: *Thinks about this for a couple of minutes. Then,* You know something? I do kind of like me. A little bit anyway. *Even though I couldn't save him. No one could save him.*

TJ: How do you feel now?

POJ: Sort of empty. And very silly.

TJ: Good. You should. Now for some homework. I want you to think about what you want to put into all that emptiness. What do you want to fill it up with?

And there it was…the rest of my life. Staring back at me from the mirror, eyebrow cocked, small grin, and a whole lot of work ahead of me.

The Joy

Photo by Pam Helling

CHAPTER THIRTEEN

My husband, the man I love above every other person on the planet, is dead. I miss him more than I could ever say. But my life is joyful.

There are a lot of parts to this joyfulness and it took a lot of effort to get here. But, here I am. And this is how I got to this place.

The steps I took along the path from deep sorrow to joy were at first unknown to me. For a while I completely bought into the standard, "Just get used to living in your new normal of grief and pain." Then one day, I did something strange…I found myself comparing my days without Ben to when I quit smoking. A super strange comparison and one that would have made Ben laugh a lot.

I had been a heavy smoker, often waking up to have a cigarette in the middle of the night. For twenty-seven years I smoked over two packs a day, so I was heavily addicted. When California made a new law that said smoking was not allowed inside any place where people worked, I went ballistic. "How on earth am I expected to choose between carrots or peas if I can't have a cigarette?" I demanded. Smoking was, of course, no longer allowed in grocery stores.

When I finally did manage to quit, I learned a lot about myself. I seem to respond to words easily, which is something I never knew before. For instance, I quickly learned that if I called myself a "former smoker" or an "ex-smoker" I would start to crave a cigarette and return to smoking. But once I started calling myself a "non-smoker" I mostly lost the urge to smoke. Non-smokers simply don't smoke and never have the urge to smoke. Ex-smokers are still smokers.

Still, those first couple of months of not smoking were total hell. I fought like crazy both to not pick up a cigarette and to come up with every excuse in the book to smoke. Not smoking eventually won out.

But in the first few weeks of being a non-smoker I would wake up every single morning and my first thought would be of how I had to somehow live through another day without a cigarette. Then I would picture a long, long road leading through the rest of my life, years and years…without a cigarette. And I would get depressed. I felt bereft, cheated, and scared. And out of control. I think it was this last thing that pushed me into doing something fairly sensible for a change.

I think that somewhere buried deep inside my psyche I have a pretty strong self-preservation instinct. I think most of us have this but are unaware of it. My self-preservation thing had already pushed one stop-smoking button and now it found another button and pushed it as well.

The first button was the decision I had made to quit smoking. Like Mark Twain, I had found quitting smoking was super easy…I had done it a thousand times. And always started up again within one or two days. But finally, self-preservation kicked in for real and I joined a Stop Smoking group that met once a week for six weeks. Of course, I initially told myself that I was joining this group to prove that it wouldn't work for me. I have no idea who I wanted to prove it to, just that I wanted to prove it to someone. Probably myself.

This group's approach to stopping smoking involved first eliminating the habit and then the physical addiction. And it wasn't easy.

I worked this program just the way they said I should except that I never once managed to not smoke when I was supposed to not smoke. I was well on the way to proving that I was destined to always be a smoker.

The last week of the program we were supposed to smoke our heads off every other day and not smoke at all the remaining days. I did just fine on the smoking days but didn't manage to get through a single one of the not-smoking days without smoking. So, at the final meeting, I planned to approach the RN who conceived and ran this program to ask her for another couple of days to get it right. I sat there and listened to the other people proudly tell their stories about successfully getting through the non-smoking days and something clicked inside my nicotine-soaked brain. I decided that I was simply playing mind games with myself and either I quit that day or I would continue smoking for the rest of my shortened life. I had to make a decision…and I did. The second button was pushed…the decision to actually quit.

That night, after the meeting, I had a little ceremony with my cigarettes and said goodbye to them. I lit my final cigarette, inhaled deeply, and just as the second hand swept across midnight, I crushed it out. I emptied the ashtray and crumbled all the rest of my cigarettes into the toilet and flushed it. And that was that. I had made the decision to not smoke.

Then started the awful mornings of facing the day without a cigarette. But also in those days were some wonders…things tasted amazing, flowers smelled so beautiful, and after a few days my coughing slowed down and eventually stopped completely. And finally, I was really and truly a non-smoker.

I still craved a cigarette every once in a while. I still do. But I long ago learned that the craving will go away whether or not I light up a cigarette. And I haven't smoked a cigarette now for thirty-six years! And I don't miss them one tiny bit.

What does my not smoking have to do with finding joy after Ben's death? Well, I was shocked when I finally connected the two things.

I had been waking up every morning since he died and my first thought was how I had to somehow live through another empty, sad day without Ben. Then I would picture a long, long road leading through the rest of my life, years and years without my Ben.

After a while this felt familiar and I tried to remember when I had experienced this before.

That self-preservation thing kicked in and I remembered that I had done this exact same thing when I quit smoking. Next, I wondered how I had gotten past those mornings back then, maybe if I did the same thing now it would help me. Of course, things tasting great and smelling terrific wasn't going to do the job. Plus, I had no interest in food and no energy to seek out flowers. And I already wasn't coughing. And a husband isn't even close to the same thing as an addiction to cigarettes. What then?

Ultimately, self-preservation kicked in again and much to my dismay I figured out that there was one thing I had done when I quit smoking that I hadn't done now. I had decided to not smoke. Maybe if I made a decision, really made a decision of some kind now, I could stop feeling like total crap.

But what decision? I had no choice about Ben, he was gone and not coming back no matter what I did. So, what needed deciding?

I played around with various things for a while, which was a first step that I didn't know I was taking. Just being willing to try made a huge difference.

Thanks to Cindy and her self-care package, I had already made the decision to start taking care of myself. And it did feel good to have clean hair again.

Thanks to Bob I had made the decision to eat real food again. And I liked doing that.

Thanks to Pam I made the decision to venture out into the world again. Okay, she dragged me kicking and screaming, but still.

And once I realized that I did want to keep living, thanks to Harold coming down with covid the day after I got lots of hugs from him, I took the next step. Harold, by the way, is a completely well person now.

I decided to be brutally honest with myself about myself and my future. This involved a series of questions that I asked myself. Questions like:

1. How many years do I reasonably have left to live? *At eighty-one years old I figured roughly ten to twenty years ahead of me. Tops.*
2. Is it possible for me to do something worthwhile with those years? *Yes, it was possible, but not easy.*
3. Did I want to do something worthwhile, or did I want to ignore life and just exist? *Given that choice, I decided that I did want to do something worthwhile. I just didn't know what.*
4. In the emotional condition I was in at that point, could I do something, anything worthwhile? *No. Not then. I was a mess.*
5. Okay then, how did I want to feel? *I wasn't sure, but I knew I didn't want to feel the way I was feeling. Sad. Lonely. Empty. Scared. Hopeless.*
6. What could I do right now, this minute, to make my future better? *I could make another decision...am I worth it? Do I have a right to feel happy even without Ben? I decided that, yes, I was worth it and, yes, I do have the right to be happy.*

And right then I conjured up a vision of Ben and the way he had always supported me. How when I was down and feeling insecure, he would point out all the ways that I was a force in the world. I thought about how much he loved me and how destroyed he would be if he ever knew that I was at the lowest point of my life because of him.

I had no right to suffer and be miserable and put all that on Ben. It certainly wasn't his fault.

So, I decided to walk down that path of life, to see where it would go, and to trust that somehow it would be all right.

CHAPTER FOURTEEN

So, I made that decision. I decided to live and to live well. To thrive. However, that was a lot easier to decide to do than to actually do.

I may have made that all-important decision, but I didn't know how to live it. I didn't know how to make it real. I still constantly pictured my gentle, kind, irreverent, fun-loving Ben lying helpless in that hospital bed. And the thought that always came next was, "I couldn't save him. I failed him when he needed me the most." And, as illogical as that thought was, it still invaded my mind several times a day. And I simply fell apart and beat myself up.

Finally, it all became too much and I started to have trouble facing the next minute let alone the next day…or the ten or twenty years I still had in front of me. So, something had to change. And change big-time.

I looked around for some way to change the way I was feeling and to change that awful picture I kept getting in my head of Ben in the hospital.

Other than my choice to stop smoking, which was aided greatly by my sense of smell and taste returning with such enthusiasm, what had I actively and successfully chosen to change my mind about in the past?

One thing, one tiny little thing crept into my awareness and that tiny little thing made all the difference. Sometimes the smallest things can make the biggest differences.

We all went through the covid lockdown, some of us more resentfully than others. Like everyone else, Ben and I longed to go out and just have breakfast at a restaurant. We wanted to go to a movie or a stage play, and we didn't like having to stay home all the time only venturing out to see the doctor or a hurried trip to a market for food. That's no way to live, but with covid raging, it was a reasonably safe way to stay alive.

I got pretty sick and tired of the lockdown thing and was getting cranky and unpleasant to be around, which I also didn't like. So, finally, I decided to do something about it. (There's that decision thing again!) I couldn't do anything at all about either covid or the lockdown, but I could do something about myself. And it was a simple little change, nothing huge or awesome, just a change in the way I was thinking about staying home.

Instead of constantly thinking, "Damn it, I have to stay home again. I can't go out." I started deliberately thinking, "Oh boy! I get to stay home again! Yay!" At first, this felt incredibly silly, but I kept at it and I said it often and aloud. Ben laughed at me, but soon he joined in and together we kept at it. "Oh boy! I don't have to go out! I get to stay home! Yay!" And eventually, this magical thing happened...we started enjoying staying home! We got to play all sorts of board games, take naps, and play with the cats. We could putter in our garden, read books, and just kick back without having to please anyone else. My little trick had worked.

But how to use that trick now? Well, what was the thing that kept invading my mind? What was the thing that broke my heart over and over again every single day? It was that mental memory of Ben in the hospital. Dying. Maybe if I deliberately changed that picture the way I had deliberately changed my lockdown thought...

Ben and I were together for thirty years. Thirty mostly wonderful years. Thirty years packed with all sorts of memories and adventures, surely there was a different picture that I could find and focus on.

I started to call up the memories. And there were tons of them! Ben and I playing Frisbee. Ben and I working together. Ben and I at various weddings. Easily a million or more pretty terrific memories to choose from.

But why choose when there were so many? Why not just call them up and let them unfold? Why not simply focus on those thirty years instead of his last day?

So, that's what I did. And it worked. I focused on the wonderful life we had shared and that took over my mind. It was almost like reliving my life with Ben. And that was a really good sprint down that path to joy.

Of course, ultimately that wasn't enough. There were still all sorts of things I had to deal with. Some of them because of the love-hate affair we all seem to have with paperwork...almost daily I had to do something legal involving Ben's death. But most of the things I still had to deal with involved just plain living.

I saw a meme on Facebook that jolted me because it was so true. I can't find it now, but this was the idea:

The death of someone you love is always hard, but losing a spouse is especially awful. The reason is that when your spouse dies everything changes. Literally everything. The way you do things changes, the way you eat, the way you sleep, how you shop, what you watch on TV, where you sit, how you talk, what you talk about, and even how you think. It's all different. And that difference is unbelievably jolting.

The complete change of everything at home is probably why the death of Springer, our cat, had hit us so hard. We lived with him and when he died, all the rhythms of our home were different. We had to learn new rhythms.

Learning a new way to live, a new way to do your day and everything in your day is hard and when you have to make those changes without your spouse, the very person you would normally turn to for help...well, then it's crushing. But it is doable. And not only is it doable, it has to be done. There is no choice. Not if you are going to continue living. And certainly not if you want to thrive.

And it's the last thing you want to do since it means he is gone. Really and truly gone.

Frankly, no one, including me, ever said any of this was easy. It isn't. But it is essential. So, if you are going to walk down that path to joy, start with baby steps.

CHAPTER FIFTEEN

A few suggestions that might make your life a little easier

It does absolutely no good at all to suppress your grief any more than it does to suppress your temper. Eventually, either one or both will burst out into public view and cause a lot of harm. Putting on a cheerful face when you feel like sobbing your heart out doesn't do you any good at all. Keeping your emotions in check in public is useful and will keep you from getting arrested, but stuffing down negative emotions all the time will do the exact opposite.

It's important to find ways of dealing with these unpleasant and potentially damaging emotions. And that can be hard to do, especially when the first words out of almost everyone's mouth is, "How are you doing today?" Usually said with a decidedly gloomy tone of voice. I found myself saying, "Oh, I'm surviving. Thanks for asking." When I just wanted to scream, "How the hell do you think I'm doing!? I feel like shit!" But we have to get through our days without someone calling the cops on us and I know that my friends were doing their damndest to be kind and gentle and to love me and care for me. But ultimately, I had to take care of myself.

Here are a few of the ways that I handled these new and often debilitating emotions. Maybe there is something here that might help you find your own path out of misery.

Now I'll admit that I do have a bit of an advantage over a lot of people...I had already lived alone for over twelve years before Ben and I got together. So, I knew how, I simply had to remember how. Of course, the world had changed a great deal in the thirty years we were together, and so had I, but not so much that I couldn't deal with it.

Right off the bat, I had to figure out how to get through days that were chock full of differences. And I had to convince my stubborn subconscious that those differences were okay. That change can be a good thing, not necessarily a scary thing. And if I find that I'm enjoying a change, enjoying something that Ben would not have cared for, that doesn't mean that I didn't really love him, or that he was wrong or I am wrong, it just means that I like something that's different. Ben and I were so close and our tastes were so alike that it sometimes surprised me that we occasionally preferred different things. But we did.

So, the first conscious, positive change that I made was with shopping for food. I bought all the things that I loved and Ben hated and I feasted on those things. And, yes, I did have to discuss this with the Guilt-Producer that lives inside of me. For instance, I had not had any chicken livers in nearly thirty years and they tasted really good. So, screw you, Guilt-Producer!

However, guilt is pretty strong and super sneaky. Guilt can land on you and take over your life before you have the slightest idea that it's even in the picture. So, you have to make a concerted effort to root guilt out and get rid of it. Get rid of unearned guilt at any rate. And regardless of anything else you might feel guilty about, guilt about the death of someone you love is unearned. Unless, of course, you hired a hit man.

The work I had done with Therapy Jill and the mirror was a good start, but now all that guilt needed to be truly eliminated not simply stuffed away into a closet somewhere inside my mind. All those painful woulda coulda shouldas kept popping up until I found a way to get rid of them that was peaceful and effective.

I got comfy and quiet and went into almost a meditative state. A few deep breaths and some conscious relaxing of the muscles in my body did the trick. Then I pictured a large basket with huge helium-filled balloons tied to the handle. Mentally I put all the different guilts that I had discovered and that were running and ruining my life into that basket. When the basket was good and full, I released it and watched as the basket containing as many guilts about Ben that I could find floated away. Farther and farther away it went until it was just a tiny dot. And finally, it disappeared over the horizon and was gone!

Guilt-Producer wasn't happy about this and quickly conjured up some more guilts and I dealt with them the same way.

I still find more guilts to deal with almost every day…Guilt-Producer is fierce and determined. But so am

I. And that basket still makes trips over the horizon. And it still works.

You may want to invent a different vehicle. I have a friend who created a raft for her guilts. She sends her guilt-laden raft over a nice, high waterfall and watches them crash at the bottom and disappear under the foaming water.

You may prefer sending your own guilts into outer space or under the sea. Or even into the sun. And you can ultimately even have some fun doing this.

With the guilts gone or mostly gone, you'll feel a bit empty. At least, I did. Something needs to fill up the empty place inside of your psyche. Guilt-Producer is always standing by ready to jump into action and fill up your emptiness. So are Bad Habits and Sloth.

For me, filling the empty space meant memories. Thirty years of memories. I filtered through them and picked several that were especially delightful and those memories are what I focused on. And I quietly relived some of my favorites.

We had been invited to a Fourth of July party by one of Ben's cousins and it was at a country club. We didn't hang out at country clubs, so this was something we were looking forward to. We also hadn't been swimming in several years, but I fished out an old swimsuit, tried it on and, wonder of wonders, it fit! So, off we went.

The country club was very busy on that holiday and it was a lovely day spent by the pool, but it was also a hot day and I finally wanted to get into the huge pool. Ben didn't feel like swimming, so I jumped in and swam around a bit then I stood up in the shallow end and called out to Ben. I'll never forget the look on his face…a mixture of shock and delight. Then he started laughing. And laughing. And laughing.

I didn't know what was so funny until his cousin's wife swam up to me and said, "Jill, you might want to pull your suit up."

I looked down and my swimsuit top was down around my waist! The suit was so old that the elastic had completely given out.

There I was in all my topless glory at a crowded pool filled with strangers and my husband was laughing his head off.

For some reason, his cousin never asked us back to that country club.

Memories of Ben helping actors learn new dialects and med students lose an accent flooded into my mind. He was so patient and so kind and gentle with his students. One young Russian, Igor, had been trying to pass his medical boards and couldn't because his accent was so strong that no one could understand him during the oral part of the exam. He was a doctor in Russia and well qualified, but that darn accent got in his way.

Ben worked with him and laughed with him and kept at it until Igor passed his boards.

Ben playing guitar and the immense concentration he put into it was a major memory as was the tingle I always felt in my spine when he sang.

I limited my memories to happy ones and avoided the last couple of years. I didn't want to remember my strong, funny, smart, kind, loving husband with dementia. So, I chose not to.

Another thing that I did, and still do, was talk to him. Aloud. About all sorts of things. The first time that I did this was when I discovered that he had not been a Blanket Thief. But after that, I talked to him about all sorts of things ranging from the answers on Jeopardy to politics.

And, for a while, this was helpful. Something that made me feel almost as though he was still here. I would shout out, "Who was Marie Antoinette?" while watching Jeopardy, then feel silly only to shout out, "What is The Grand Canyon?" a few minutes later.

Now, although I do still talk to him, I do it less and less. However, it does still help a little bit.

Just as I went through a little ceremony when I finally quit smoking, I know that I will have to do the same when it comes time to let Ben go. I'm not quite there yet, I'm still getting used to being alone and getting over liking being alone.

"You're liking the freedom of being alone, that means you didn't really love Ben, you know." Oh, shut up, Guilt-Producer! It doesn't mean that at all. And I have a nice, big basket all ready to dump your stupid guilts into, so bring 'em on!

Any time you make a change in your life, you have to make some adjustments.

Big change, big adjustments. We don't think all that much about the adjustments we make as we maneuver through our lives, we just do it. Adjusting becomes automatic. Until something comes along that is the mother of all changes. Something like the death of someone who meant everything to you. When that happens, at first you flounder. You live in a fog of sorrow without really interacting with anything or anyone around you.

And that can become your "new normal" if you're not careful. Once you're in that fog, it becomes way too easy to stay there. Climbing out of the fog means hard work and some pain and you've just been through so much pain. Inviting more pain into your life is the last thing you want to do.

But if you want to do more than simply exist, climbing out of the safe, comfortable fog is essential. And it's also essential that you *want* to make the needed adjustments. You must want to embrace your new life, ultimately with gusto and joy.

That's the secret to leaving your sorrow behind…wanting to be happy again. Differently happy, but still happy.

So, here are some of the steps that I took that have helped me and might help you as well.

- Confronting my sadness and the horror of losing the love of my life. Facing it squarely and without fear.
- Finding the courage to decide to find joy without him. Finding a way to do this will come later, the important thing is making the decision.
- Doing mirror work. Discovering or creating Therapist Jill and working with her. Even though TJ was often obnoxious and difficult, I trusted her because she was, after all, me.
- Dealing with guilt and understanding that guilt will keep showing up over and over. And that's just fine

as long as I can implement a way to deal with my Guilt-Producer. My basket-and-balloons seem to work nicely.

- Without pushing or hiding the bad stuff deep down inside of myself where it can fester, choosing instead to focus on the good. The memories of Ben and our life together.

- Choosing joy as a way of life and letting it come to me. Knowing that it will.

- Understanding that my being happy again is a wonderful way of honoring Ben since the last thing he would ever want for me would be unrelenting sadness. Especially since he was filled with laughter and joy.

CHAPTER SIXTEEN

So, there it is, my path to joy. And, guess what? I'm still walking along that path and still climbing over the odd boulder. Do I miss my Ben? Oh, yes! More than I could ever have thought possible...but I no longer dwell on missing him. Instead, I enjoy the thirty years of wonderful memories that I shared with him and I find myself looking forward to tomorrow. And to next year. And the year after that. All the new memories that I'm going to make and enjoy.

And I'm even working on a way to collaborate with Guilt-Producer so that we might someday work together and be friends. It's either that or find some way to strangle the miserable SOB! And frankly, the latter option is the most appealing!

I hope that something in this little book has resonated with you and perhaps helped you find a new way of living in the world. A way that has joy in it. And sunshine.

As my friend Bob said:
"Coping skills are a form of defeat. Getting back in the sunshine is a victory."

Ben with two of his favorite things…
cats and a book

ABOUT THE AUTHOR

Jill was born into a show-biz family and raised in Hollywood. She has had many careers in her life including her own radio talk-show and a decade as a Motion Picture ADR Editor. She won an Emmy for her work on the 1984 TV Movie, *The Day After*. For the past 30 years she has worked, with her husband, Ben, as a Standardized Patient in the Simulation Programs of three different medical schools. Jill is now retired and lives in Oregon with two cats.

Made in the USA
Las Vegas, NV
12 November 2022